ELIZABETH W. GREENLEAF
A Bird's-Eye View

Notes from the Publisher

Composers In Focus is a series of original piano collections celebrating the
creative artistry of contemporary composers. It is through the work of these
composers that the piano teaching repertoire is enlarged and enhanced.

It is my hope that students, teachers, and all others who experience this music
will be enriched and inspired.

Frank J Hackinson

Frank J. Hackinson, Publisher

Notes from the Composer

Watching birds has always been a favorite hobby of mine. This book of "birdsongs"
is about some of their interesting habits and experiences. I hope you have a great
time imagining life in birdland!

Elizabeth W. Greenleaf

Elizabeth W. Greenleaf

Contents

Crow Talk

Two crows are talking to each other.
They are joking about how silly the farmer's scarecrow looks.

Elizabeth W. Greenleaf

Busily

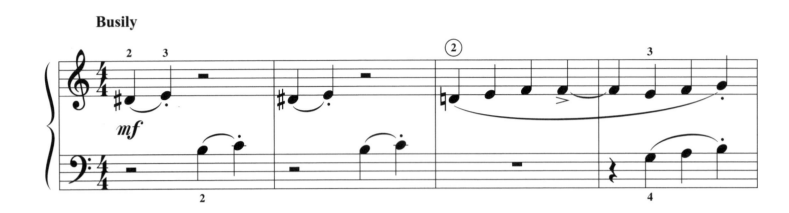

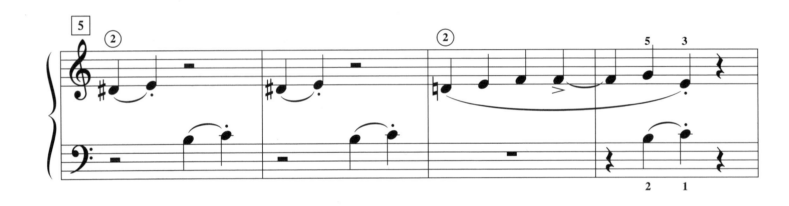

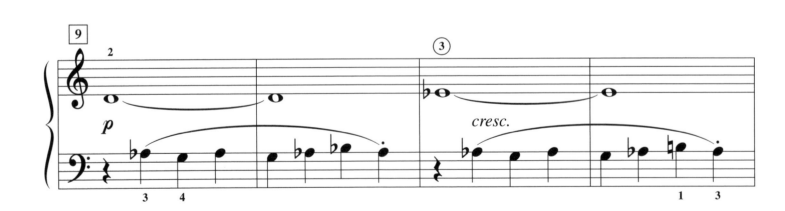

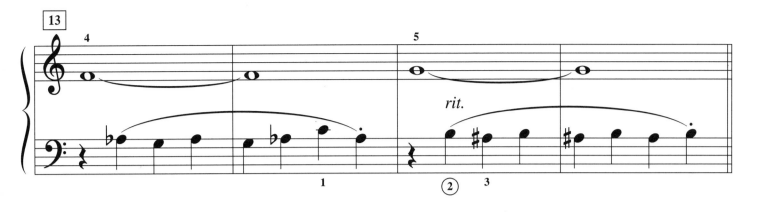

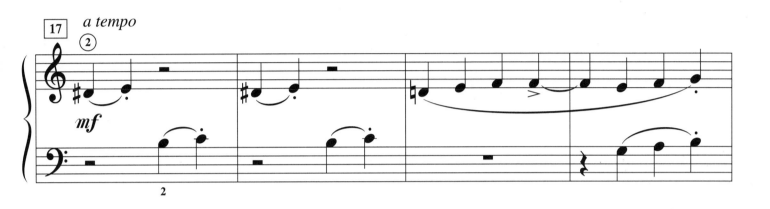

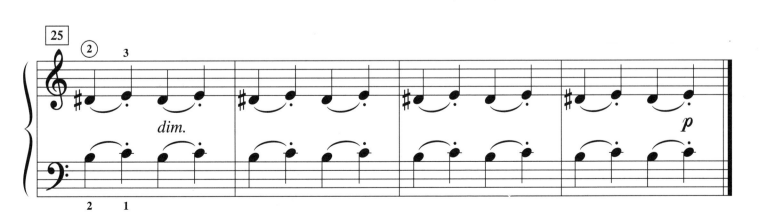

Asleep in the Nest

This is a restful piece about baby birds dozing after being fed a tasty meal.

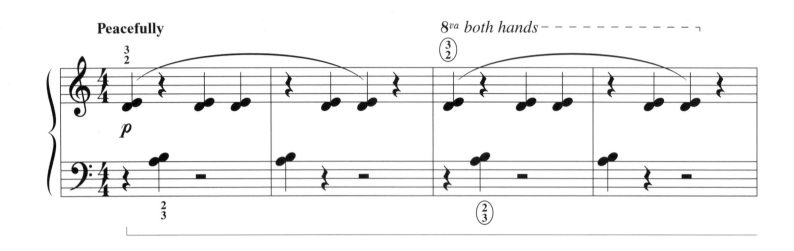

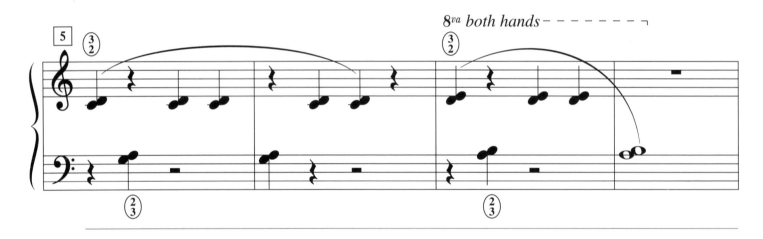

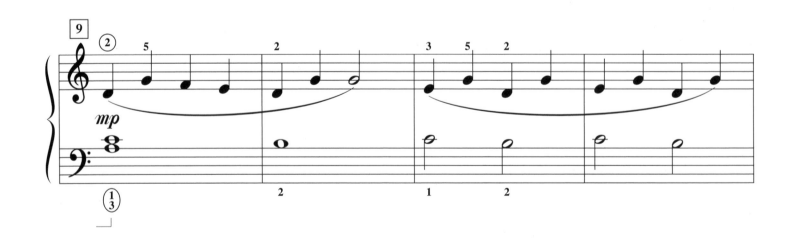

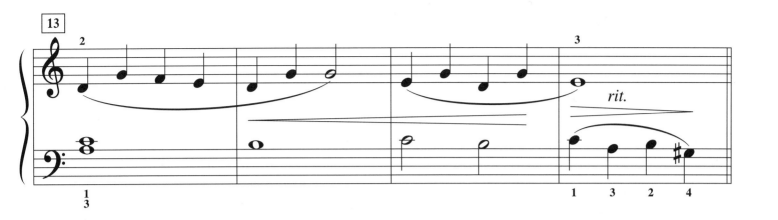

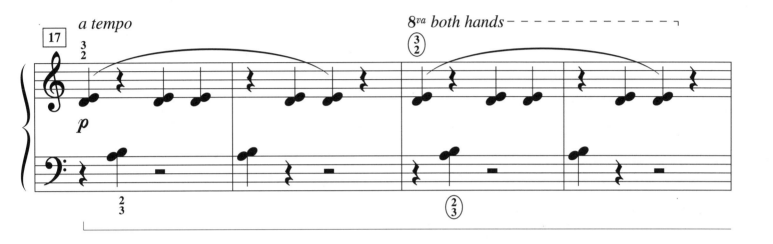

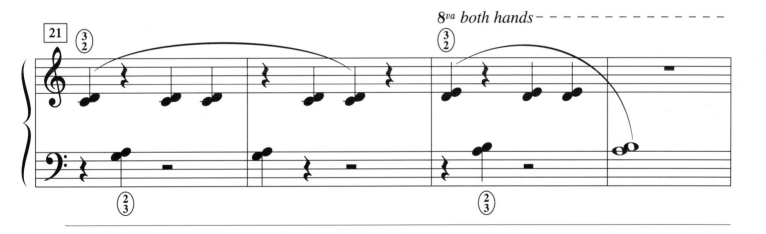

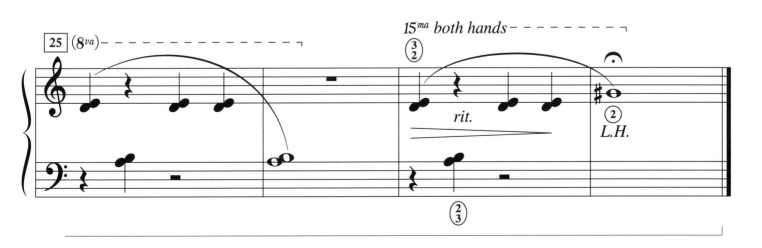

March of the Penguins

Imagine the back-and-forth waddle of penguins as they march along the cold terrain.

Briskly

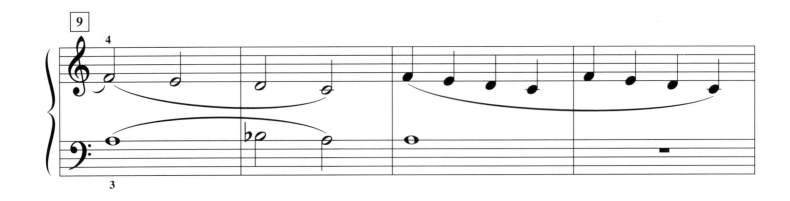

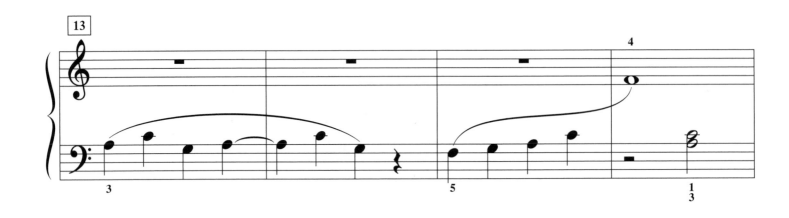

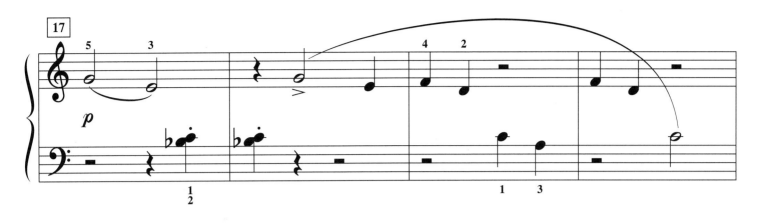

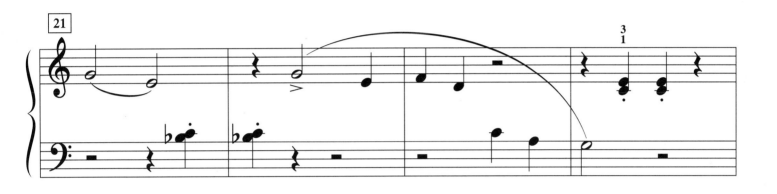

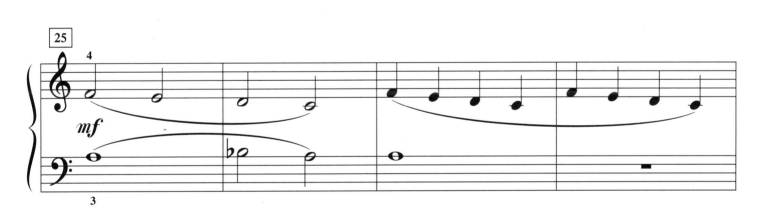

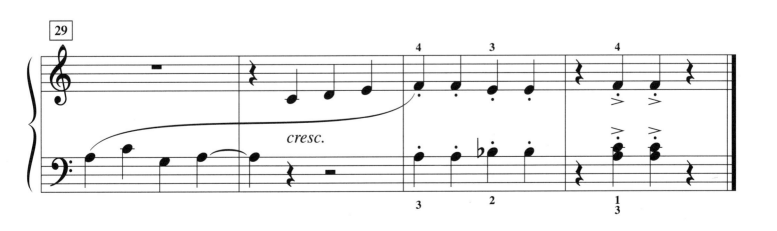

A Feather in the Breeze

A pretty feather twirls and swirls gracefully in the wind.

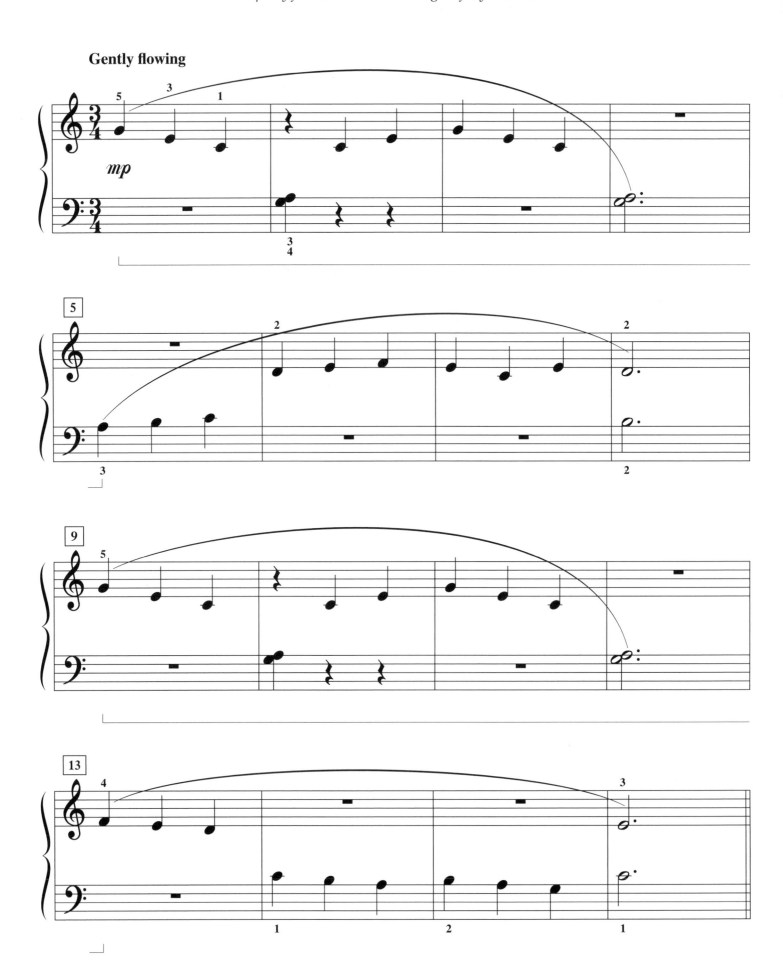

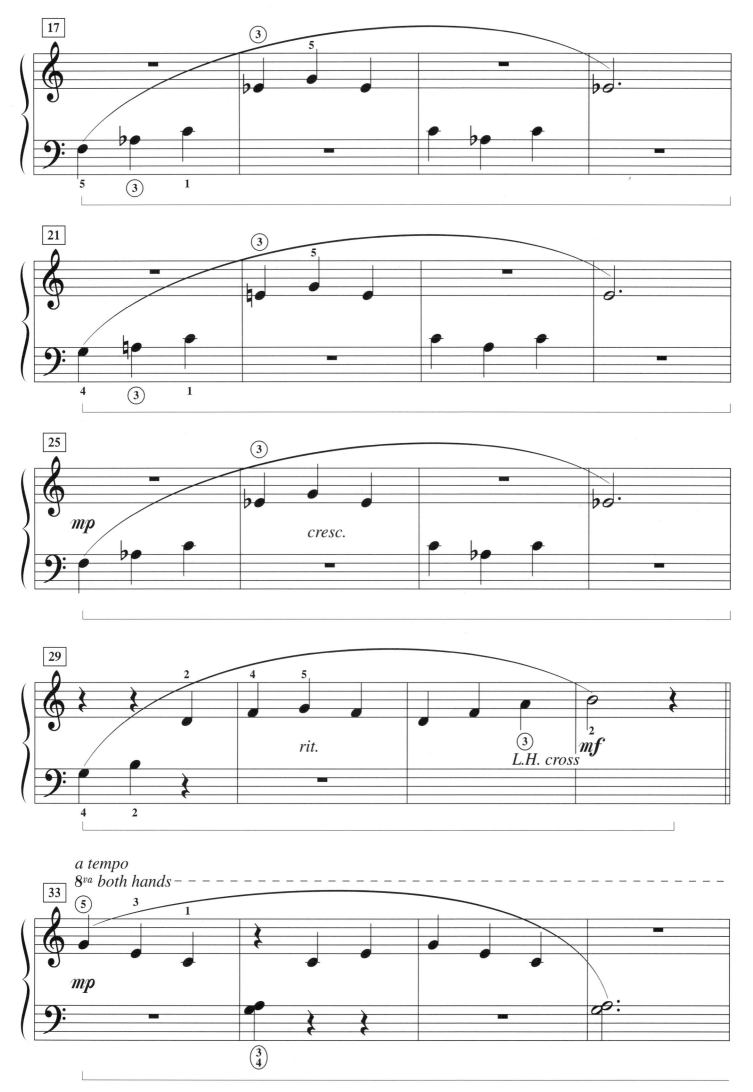

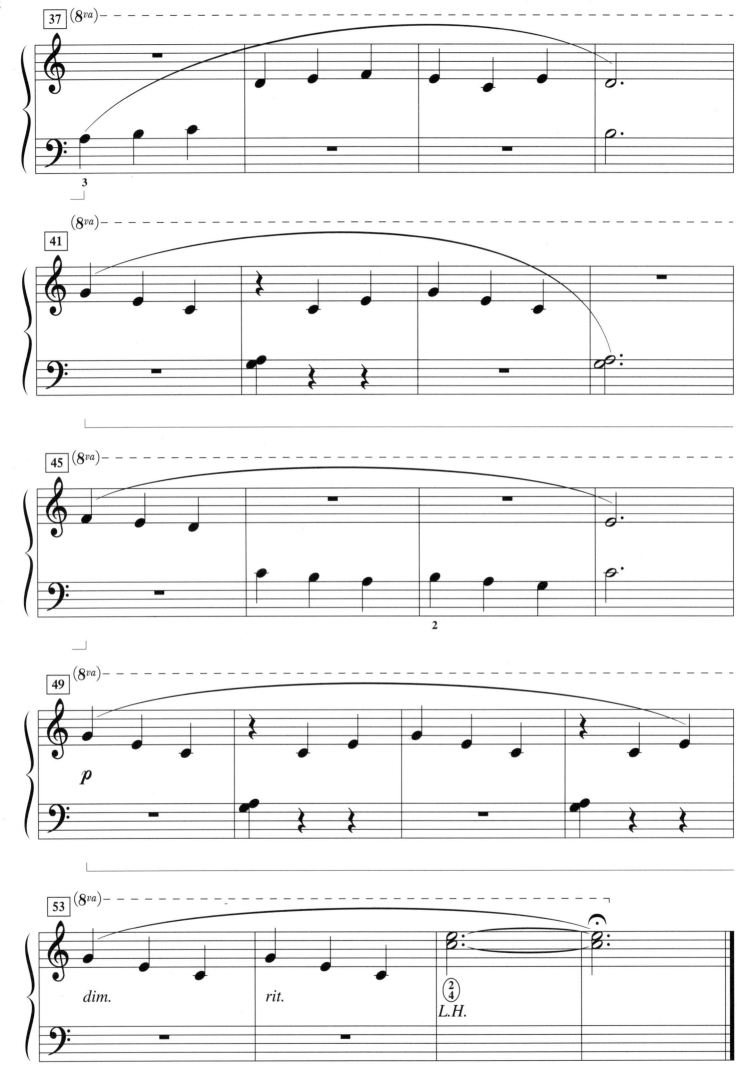

The Mournful Worm

This worm is sad because he lost a brother to a hungry bird.

The Silly Sandpiper

This sandpiper looks silly with its head low and tail bobbing up and down.
It pecks for food along the sandy shore.

Happily

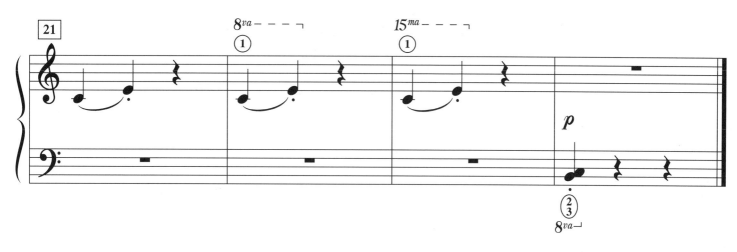

Songbird Chorus

Imagine the sound of many birds singing in a lush forest.

Chirpily

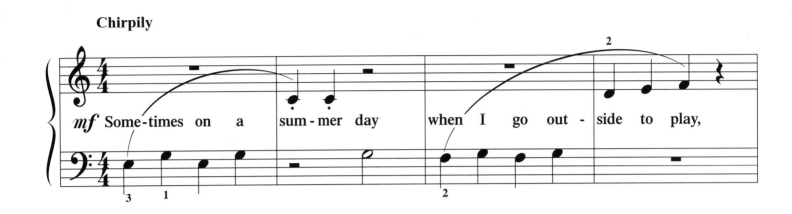

Some-times on a sum-mer day when I go out - side to play,

I can hear such cheer-ful sounds, song-birds sing - ing all a - round.

Loud and clear they chirp and trill, say - ing "Hi!" to all.

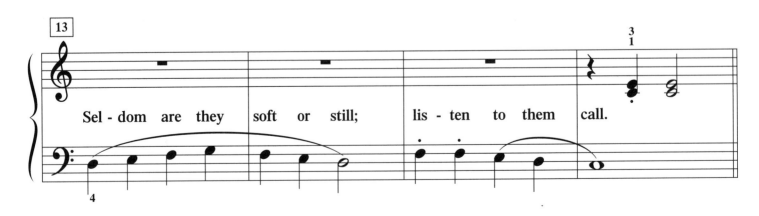

Sel - dom are they soft or still; lis - ten to them call.

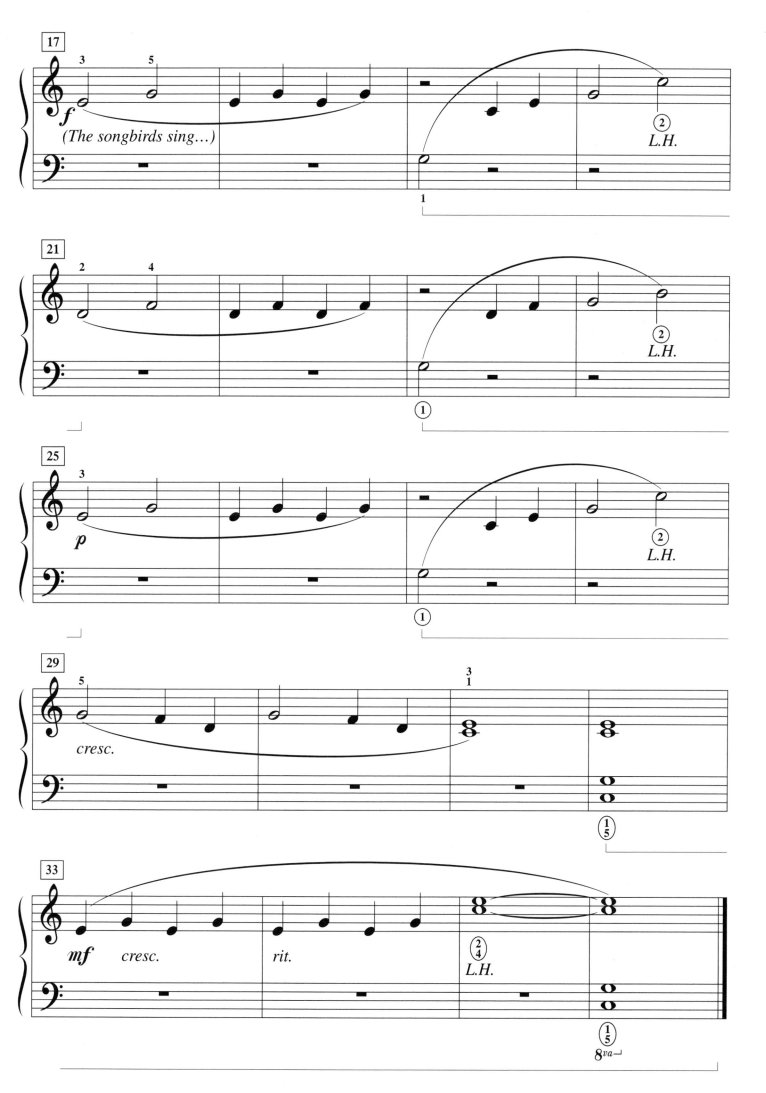

Struttin' Turkey Blues

This turkey is big, beautiful, and proud.
He struts to attract the hens nearby.

With a swinging beat* ($\half$ = ca. 126)

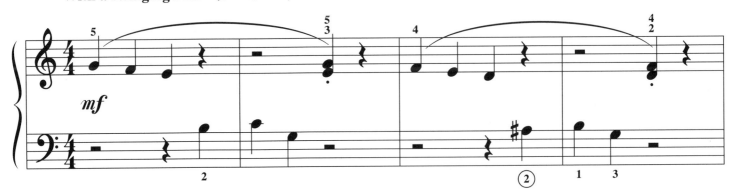

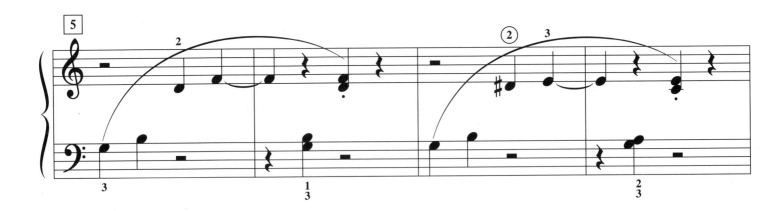

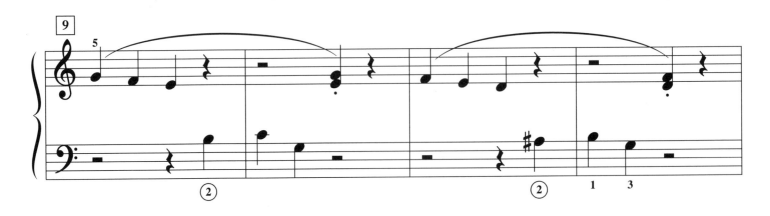

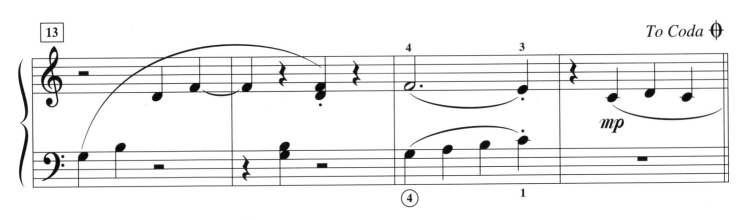

*May be played in swing rhythm ($\quarter \quarter = \eighth^3\eighth$)

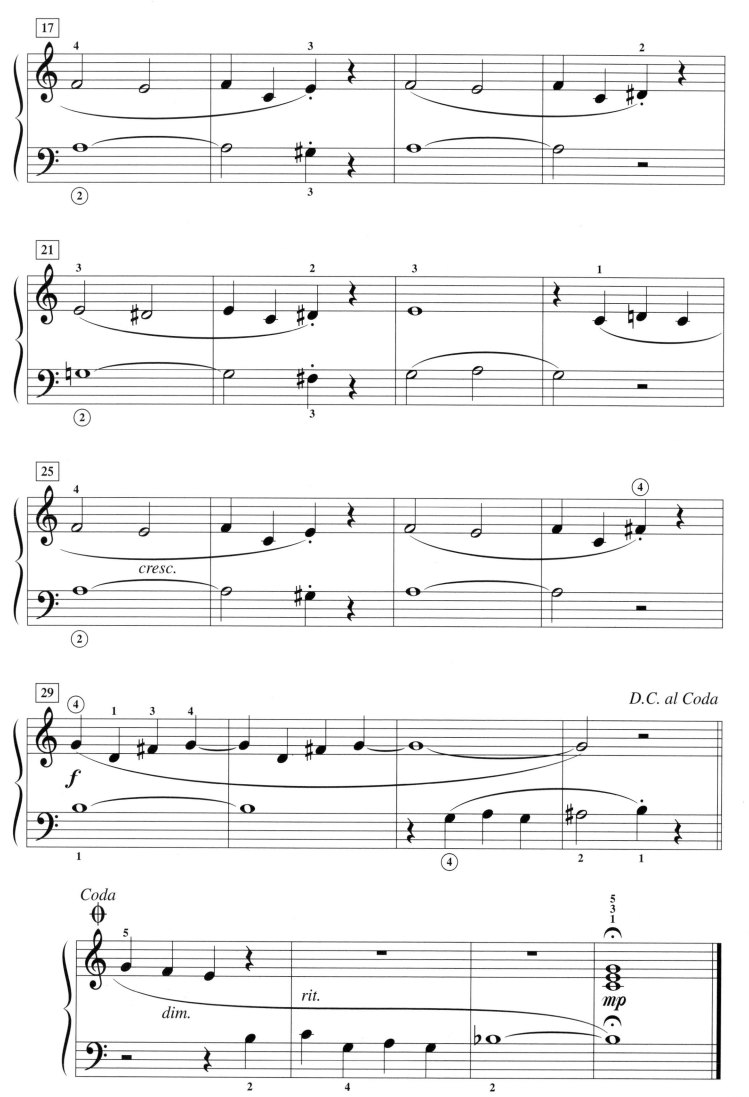

Cat Attack!

A cat is sneaking up to attack a bird.
Where in the music do you hear a pounce?

Sneaky and quick

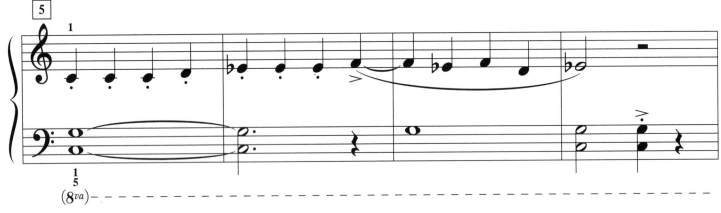

21

FF1364

The Chicken Pecks for Dinner

A chicken roams the yard, scratching and pecking for food.

Briskly